THRESH & HOLD

Thresh & Hold

Marlanda Dekine

HUB CITY PRESS
SPARTANBURG, SC

Book design: Meg Reid
Cover design: Kate McMullen
Cover Image: "Westward, 2016"
© Fletcher Williams III
Author Photo: Tam Marie

TEXT Adobe Garamond 11/15
DISPLAY HK Grotesk 15/13.4

Library of Congress
Cataloging-in-Publication Data

Dekine, Marlanda, author.
Thresh & hold / Marlanda Dekine.
Other titles: Thresh and hold
Spartanburg, SC : Hub City Press
Berkeley, CA : Distributed to the trade by Publishers Group West, [2022]
Identifiers: LCCN 2021057410
ISBN 9781938235948 (paperback)
ISBN 9781938235955 (epub)
Subjects: LCGFT: Poetry.
Classification:
LCC PS3604.E377 T48 2022
DDC 811/.6—dc23/eng/20211213
LC record available at https://lccn.loc.gov/2021057410

Hub City Press gratefully acknowledges support from the National Endowment for the Arts, the Amazon Literary Partnership, South Arts, and the South Carolina Arts Commission.

HUB CITY PRESS
200 Ezell Street
Spartanburg, SC 29306
1.864.577.9349

TABLE OF CONTENTS

for Imagination

THE BLACK RIVER

whispered dreams   spanish moss reached   when we moved back
to where my parents grew up I was eating more rice than I knew
existed and I did not want to be
up and down   the village is known as Jackson Village Road

I didn't understand   home   why   people   were
speaking to me in   home   stories
telling me   home
which of our dead   home   I resembled
home   so many cousins
I had   home   and so many questions for
God
I have never prayed   home   as much as I
home
home
wonder
home
home
home

I

Look. The tree of our hands is for all.
It is converting the wounds which were cut in its
trunk
the soil works
and among the branches heady sweet blossoms of haste

–Aimé Césaire, *from Cahier d'un retour au pays natal*

ORIGIN

I was born on a fourth Sunday to my first-lady Grandma Thelma,
my dark-skinned roll of hickory thigh meat and eyes
disturbed her. She rubbed Ambi skin fade cream
into my face to bless me.

I heaved for my petrified ma
who would not cry.
My father, my dark-skinned hope.

In his arms, I was cloaked. Beneath stars
my mother's mothers, my father's fathers worked,
we were given a French last name, Dekine.

Chartreuse blades of grass grew out of the spaces
between their toes. The musty air filled with songs,
my throat moans mimicking nightingales
from the old-world.

I AM BOUND FOR DE KINGDOM

—after Florence Price and Marian Anderson

My granddaddy Silas was born on the Nightingale plantation
in Plantersville, South Carolina on riverbanks that loved
three generations of my kin, captured
in a green-tinted photograph, hanging in my daddy's den.

Tonight, my eyes will take each old-world bird from the cropped space,
send them home with their songs and favorite foods.

Look out for me I'm a-coming too

with rice, okra, hard-boiled eggs, and Lord Calvert.
My daddy says if I get out of my car on Nightingale land,
the folks who own it might shoot. My daddy says,
"Never leave the driveway."

Glory into my soul

I watch all of my ascendants. Their faces reflecting me
in that photograph. Their eyes are dead
black-eyed Susans.

FIRST LADY OF THE CHURCH

I don't want to remember
how she made the reverend run,

praying scriptures
like spells while sitting

next to peace lilies.
So many times I was afraid

of her searching for camphor,
her tales of the plat-eye

and hags, burning pine needles all while laughing
at the audacity of wayward men.

Grandma Thelma turned trees into so many things.
She'd disappear into grapevines unbothered by snakes,

return with her brown hands, purple and wet.
She mashed muscadines into wine

like her eight children: graduations, marriages,
her own ever-widening family tree.

Grandma Thelma stayed humming
and telling folk how God come fa we.

She called my Grandpa Mose
because everybody knows he knew God,
she knew his hands flung her face

into red sea blues. His voice shook pews,
he came for my grandmother,

his hands took her tooth.
Grandma Thelma told me

I bit e finger
in two.

I just know when I couldn't go
to school

with my fever, I'd awaken
safely—next to the warmth

of her woodstove, and she was healing me.

IF ANYBODY ASKS YOU WHAT'S THE MATTER WITH ME

When I was eleven years old my ma dropped me
at my daddy's family graveyard and drove away.

If I kept worrying it's where I'd end up, she said.
Terrified, I hid from my last name like a purple lizard
beneath a magnolia leaf.

I crossed the road marking my distance,
I put my hands in my pockets, hummed
Running for My Life.

I didn't want to point, I tried
to avoid the engraved D,
I tried not to smell my Grandma Lizzie's perfume,
moth balls rising from the dirt.
I listened to the chickadees around me.

Today I drove
myself to our family graveyard,
with my windows slightly ajar, I watched

smoke fleeing from my cigar.
I'm sliding in no mo struggle.
I got out

I poured one for my Aunt Angie.

A ROSE

In a dream my daddy found his ma hanging
one night inside a bedroom closet.

She'd been dead
thirteen years. I was asleep
and nine years old.

He said her mouth was a cave opening.
Inside there was a choir of deacons,
dressed and ready for the ritual,
a trilling crescendo of sweet songs,
nightingales who wanted
to be filled by forgiveness, singing

She 'rose

She arose from the deeeeeeead

Grandma Lizzie cued the choir.
They dragged my daddy in that last note.
Every bird moaned at once,
"E gon be jes like e daddy!"

I watch turkey vultures gather over my family's field.
Why we let nothing die
easily?

HURRICANE FAMILY

When hurricanes come my daddy prepares
by rooting soles into the floors of our house,
rooted into the wetland his daddy poured Lord Calvert into.

No longer a buckra's sharecropper,
Grandma Lizzie and Granddaddy Silas rooted
a bottle tree of twelve
inconceivable indigo children.

My daddy repeats to my ma,
We'll be fine,
and I believe.

When the hurricanes came, it moved me
more than I wanted. I hooked my innocence inside.
Wild water became swords. My sisters and I played in
swooning pine. Dark, slick, splash, and I was terrified—

my thoughts of trees falling on top of mobile homes,
people waking with blue Earth inside their rooms,
worlds swept up for miles out all around,

and in our front yard—I was afraid
while we ran, we danced, and we leaped.

MY GRANDMA TOLD STORIES OR CAUTIONARY TALES

Grandma Thelma told me if I slept on my back,
a hag would ride me and I'd never return, so I trained
my body to sleep on my stomach. Even now,
if I wake up cold, I open my mouth
and repeat the 23rd Psalm.

Grandma Thelma told me I might see a plat-eye
when I was seven years old. I could imagine
cypress knees growing full bodies
to walk the hungry road, an entire body
of eye nicknamed Plat.

Grandma Thelma told me I'd feel welcomed by the eye.
I'd be made to feel safe and loved,
but if I looked directly into that big white-bodied cornea,
I'd forget where I came from.
I'd be disappeared.

WE OPENED THE BOX TUCKED WAY BACK IN THE CLOSET

Discovered books
of flat-tabbed clothing
and bodies of burnt umber,
pale, and olive hues.

Ma saved paper dolls
from her childhood.

My sisters and I couldn't imagine
our serious mother, the math teacher,
playing with paper dolls,
without becoming knots
of laughter and jokes.

Beneath them, a folder
of love poems
written by our daddy.

They'd been rewritten
by our ma, with bouquets
of flowers sketched
around prose
in red, pink, and purple
were the words

love   love   love

MY BLACK, RURAL, QUEER CHILDHOOD

I want my body, but I don't
want it to be called a body
reminds me of when
my family and I were driving
through Manning, South Carolina   I was the first to see
the big black sound   the buzzing in all our ears   I'd never heard
of a horsefly
I just knew it was big

    I screamed
and our big brown caravan stopped
at a triangular median
smack dab in the middle of a small downtown road   I screamed
The horsefly buzzed and smacked itself
into the wide windows of blue sky   I don't remember

I can spot a single ant on a dark surface

Maybe I've been afraid
to claim my body, afraid to be wild

                        and breakout into all this sky   around me

Perhaps I can burst

    through ceilings and glass,   explode into joy?

NON-LINEAR

My Grandma Thelma taught me to wash my face
and my ma was my first English teacher.

I knew how to read and write by age three
because Grandma Thelma was forced
to quit school.
My ma fed me language like grits
and called me a good, smart child.

When I left, I did not
have to be good.
I only had to love what I love.

When I was eight, I asked my ma
why the world went black
when I closed my eyes,
where did everything go?

Two weeks after I was born,
Grandpa Mose told her,
Feed em and e'll grow. Das it.

After college, we walked together
on a bike path near my first
bachelor apartment.
Ma said it was a quick four hours away from her.
If something happened, she could get to me.

She said I was walking too slow.
I was watching the wind
pick hair from my Labrador's coat.
I saw my mother and her feet next to mine,
inflamed like her ma's.
I was like a child when we got back to my apartment.
She asked me to take off her shoes.

POLICE IN PLANTERSVILLE ELEMENTARY SCHOOL

made
my ma tuck
her children in a crevice
of her mind, inside our yellow home
of windows that did not open,
safe from kin
stolen by a white   thing in the night.

made
my daddy watch
beloveds and family   fiend
convulse   die
lies beneath a moon he dreams under

                                        he knew
                                        crack wasn't shipped
                                        by Blacks.

made
me an 80's baby singing,
D-I won't do Drugs!
A-Won't have an Attitude!
R-I will Respect myself!
E-I will Educate me!

MA

I watched my mother
learn to walk again
after surgeries on each knee
over the course of six months.

She kicked me out of her house,
because I was an unforgiving mirror.

My ma loves me more than
she ever learned to love herself.

I witnessed her realize
a monarch butterfly sat on the porch
for thirty minutes of her company.

When the first knee reintegrated,
my ma remembered everything
that ever hurt and the root. Tales

of surviving a tsunami
of a father and a hardened mother
she loved, how she forgives them at the graveyard
with tears and flowers.

My ma,
my love, is always teaching me.

She knows pain I cannot write. I no longer hold.
I go to the water.

My ma, I love. My rose,
my thorn. I will never leave,
even when I leave.

My ma is every sinew
of my every muscle, everything
I have ever done. My heartbeat loves her
being.

My ma, the fixer.
And, the butterflies!
Oh, the sweet butterflies
that move us closer
to our true natures.

My ma would not rest,
but she's learning

I'm right here, ma.
I'm right here.

JACKSON VILLAGE ROAD

You grew from your granddaddy's dirt
and evergreen spaces.

There are gorgeous collard colored-greens, ripe
yellows turning to golden reds, hanging
from brown and moss-smothered trunks, standing tall
all over the land he left.

A Black man, last name Jackson, quietly purchased
land from a white man and sold acres of unworkable plots
to your great-granddaddy.

Your granddaddy, Silas, filled the swamp
with dirt gathered from the woods he slept beneath
as a runaway child.

On the south side of his house is where he used to plant.
His brain
was a farmer's almanac scrabbled with voices and visions.
This, too, is your inheritance.
His greens reached and sprawled
beyond his containers, spilling into all his children's
kitchen sinks.

His mother and the life in his eyes died
when he was ten years old. Your granddaddy was already
all different kinds of blue

reaching   spreading

going   on   and   on   and   on

talking to people   he could not see.

DADDY, THE DREAMER

When you picked red azaleas for Grandma Lizzie,
did jokes smother you in front of your boys?

Did granddaddy Silas call you stupid
as quickly as he'd pick up his gun
and point it towards your face,
his own reflection?

Before the world shouted what would make you
into a real man, I chose you
because you are water.

When I was born, you were running behind,
but you'd already dreamt my first name.

MY DADDY GAVE ME BRANDY WHEN I TURNED SIXTEEN

See how nasty it is? Don't drink, he said.

When I was 20, I visited home
with my red Solo cup and new shoulder blades,
cutting my tank top.

I wanted to be just like my daddy.
I'd been lifting reps

the way he did before we moved back
to Plantersville.
He couldn't stand his friends
seeing me this way.
When I couldn't stand his shame,

I'd go
looking for my little brother.
I'd go
find which tree he is at.
Either at *Up Jump the Devil*
or at *Cross the Branch,*
somewhere our ma said not to plant
himself.

I'd find him and find myself
sitting with our
inherited shadows.

THE SHADE TREE

You will find me in every Gullah-Geechee place,
holy haunting I watch.

I get to know who visits me
I want to be a good psychic
            I celebrate the gathering of water

                  I love to   breathe   the
                                 air   they   breathe
I watch Tre roll a blunt

Dereese push pleasure smoke
while all her folk are moved
by her spirit
                  sweet

                      tobacco   wafting headstones

CHILDHOOD LESSONS FROM THE GIRL NEXT DOOR

She was standing at the top of our family road, watching
me dribble. I'm not sure if she was watching,
but I didn't want her to see me seeing her
so I kept pounding the asphalt with the sun.

I held it in my palm and tried to spin its rays
on my index finger
and failed. I tried no more tricks.
I would not dare take a shot.

She walked over, took the heat from my hands, my body.
She showed me how to do a crossover,
over and over again.
Her dark cocoa legs crisscrossing wildfire.

Her forehead curling
inward, right before,
she reached to give me back
the ball.

WHEN THE PREACHER WAS GOD

I am likely drawn
        to those who are making
                love in the chaos.
I probably am catapulted

        by all things terrifying me.
            I have a reason for being.
                    I draw each point up
                    until now. I return home

dressed in purple and gold, waiting to take
        my Grandma Thelma's violet church hat
out for lunch. I can't keep up

        with her hat remembering all the thoughts she had
        while Grandpa Mose was up in that pulpit,
                    making people run.
        I remember those summers,

hiding with my Sega Genesis, dreading their church's
        children's bible week where a loving girl ran up on me
        and said,
            You! I'ma fight you!

and a cornfield full of her cousins ears heard and taunted
            Ooooooo!

I hid behind my Grandpa Mose
        clergy door.
When he found out why, he laughed,
        told me to go out and play.

Something he had never allowed me to do.
        At first, I did not stand when his voice boomed
over our peppermint drunk bodies,
                Are there any visitors in the church today?

Pew-perched and drenched,
        I'd just returned from battle in his churchyard
beneath God's unrelenting sun.

        I did not stand
until he gave me a look
        that made me.

COLLECTING MYSELF

I opened the door and all the girls were gone.
No one was peeking into my bathroom stall anymore.

No one asked me if I am a boy today.
It was just me

sitting on a cold floor, waiting to open my eyes.
I imagined their spit was river water shined by moon.

I could drink from it. Their laughter
bloomed into my

bloody noses.
I loved all the girls.

The closest I got to one of them was in 4th grade
P.E. when India aimed

the baseball and caught me hard in my eye.
She ran over before the teacher could see,

and she searched my face for blood.
I waited for her to pick me up

like I belonged to her.

THRESH & HOLD

Flooding in now, I rest
so I can harvest new worlds,
a ready net so still.

Without rest, I cannot hear
my Grandma Lizzie and my Grandma Thelma. Without rest,
I cannot hear my Aunt Carolyn composing for her Lord.
I cannot hear my Aunt Angie cussin
angels while guiding me across memoried waters.

I am learning what *real* power is.

A year ago, I wouldn't have
felt our bright red, black, green chords of spirit calling.
Women in my family have dropped dead one day
and the family kept right on working.

I rest like I have tomorrows
growing on a vine outside. I rest
like a horned owl.

My ancestors turned into machines
by *rice is booming in Georgetown, sale extravaganza!*
I rest beneath my Grandma Lizzie's oil-dressed magnolia
painted white and green at the trunk. I risk surrender to her dark
sashay.

West Africa caught my granddaddy Silas by the brain.

Here's a cosmos I picked
from his field of grasses. Women in my family
have dropped dead one day, purple-gowned
and waiting for us in the next.

PERHAPS I AM A FUGITIVE OF EMPATHY

Vigilant for so long,

I am full.   There are centuries

of terror crawling just beneath my skin.

I no longer consider anyone's noise as my noise.

I care for Henrietta Lacks
and all the names whispered
in my ear by the live
oak trees.

I don't care about   the father of modern gynecology,
honored on South Carolina's golf course capitol.

Memory floods
when I walk on grasses   because white clovers pushed honey
while Black penises fell upon them.

I think of which bodies
have saved bodies
without permission,
without mutuality.

I think of Black

bodies that didn't make it
off the bloody table.

So, I don't die
at the hands of myself standing in the shoes of whiteness,

I've been dancing with my Spirit
beneath old cedars.

I've been building my imagination
by visiting with feral cats.
I've been burying my feet in the dirt,
staring at magnolia trees, and counting waves
in the Atlantic.

Exhausted of singing in   an empire's hopeful choir,

I've been sitting with my grandmas
in their photographs,
while wafting frankincense and myrrh,
and I've been thinking
about what Giovanni said to Baldwin
in that resurfaced interview on the language of love:

if you don't understand yourself,
you don't understand anybody else.

III

A HOLY PLACE

When I'd enter Bethel A.M.E.
tucked into the elbow
of Jackson Village Road,
I wanted to be more
quiet than quiet was
because inside, the walls
were golden. I'd smell Pine-Sol and
fried chicken, hear rice boiling, babies
crying and elders moaning.
I was afraid of something dark
and powerful I felt and did not understand.

Ms. Ruby led the women's choir
and could cuss you back to your maker.
Every Sunday,
magicians showed up,
turning bodies bent by work and grief
into bolts of lightning,
ringing out shouts
until the old timbered floor quaked
beneath my feet.

Thirteen year old, Rev. Young,
would preach until faces were honey-drenched
with relief. I didn't know
all those hallelujahs and amens,
church ladies humming
and waving fans meant free.

A golden bell, its long white rope,
children running around the church steeple
on a red-brick porch, covered in crimson suede,
the purple sky like someone built it around Bethel.

WHEN I BUILD

I remind myself
it is not more of our stories that will build a bridge.
I only have one back,
and it is mine until I die.

I show up and let my mouth
    run free as the Black River,
       blow people away while rice fields flood
          what's been forgotten with blood,
             let people figure out what happened,

I collect the check.
I am from people with their feet on the ground,
heads in whole other worlds.

WHY WE SAY "THE VILLAGE"?

Maybe, it's because the crossroads
inside Annie and Jackson
Village Road's cheek bones dimple is our mutual
aid and our Southern star.

Perhaps, it's how we land-
marked us, where our people
been since before the 1800s.

Maybe, it's because of the dirt road loops
with names like Ezra and Ephesians
connecting heir's property and our beautiful
cinder block gardens of black-eyed Susans.

Maybe, it's because we sit
beneath shade trees that giggle
in the wind at night.

Perhaps, the village is a lighthouse
in centuries long of dark. The reason might be the plight,
being that *Negro Friend* so your kin stays alive
for the next three centuries, might be the right
to take up space and name it what we want,
remembering,
remembering,
emembering,

we the village,
the family,
worked, kept, and loved
this land.

PREFACE*

~~Georgetown County, South Carolina, was first seen by white men in 1526, almost four and a half centuries ago and a mere thirty-four years after the famous voyage of Christopher Columbus. However, the Spanish left no visible remains during their brief sojourn. Not even subtle traces, such as place names, are left to mark their attempted settlement.~~

~~Until the English arrived in the early 1700's, the Georgetown region was~~ the land of ~~the Indians~~. These peoples, ~~too, made few permanent impressions on the area, but some Indian~~ names ~~have lasted through the years:~~ the bay - Winyah; the rivers - Sampit, Pee Dee, Waccamaw, Santee; ~~and some plantations~~ - Hopsewee, Chicora Wood, Wachesaw.

~~From the eighteenth and nineteenth centuries, however, there is a considerable number of~~ tangible reminders of the past in Georgetown County. ~~This inheritance has irresistible appeal to a legion of Americans today as the thriving second half of the twentieth century rushes along at a frenzied pace.~~

~~The appeal of Georgetown County touches~~ the native ~~and the new arrival alike. Elma Harrelson is a native, an employee of the International Paper Company, and a photographer by avocation. Dennis Lawson is an historian by training who came to Georgetown just before the Tricentennial to serve as~~

* West and Central Africans, enslaved African people, and Black people are not mentioned

~~Director of The Rice Museum.~~

~~That such a booklet as *A Goodly Heritage* was needed was a foregone conclusion when these two individuals met. "*Elma's Georgetown County,*" an exhibition of more than one hundred photographs of the area taken by Miss Harrelson and shown at The Rice Museum from April 9 through May 15, 1972, reinforced the desire for such a publication.~~

~~Discussions between Mr. Lawson and Charles A. Moore, Vice President for Georgetown of the South Carolina National Bank and a citizen most~~ conscious of the history of ~~his community, secured the financial basis for the undertaking.~~

~~By photograph and descriptive text, this pamphlet illustrates the history of Georgetown County as seen by the tangible evidences of its past from the 1700's into the twentieth century. Almost without exception, every structure shown within these pages can be visited today. Few are the communities in these United States which have such a physical legacy from their past.~~

Georgetown County ~~is a~~ land of live oaks and Spanish moss, ~~an area bountifully endowed by Providence, and a region prospering from twentieth century industrialization. Above all else, this portion of the Low Country has retained *A Goodly Heritage*.~~

PLANTERSVILLE, SOUTH CAROLINA

I take the Winyah Bay on a Tour de Plantersville. The local Rice Museum would like to come, but it cannot until its donors complete the following: 1) Pamphlets & videos denote that the natives were not European discoverers, 2) Its ticketed events acknowledge the enslaved West & Central Africans stolen to build a third of the nation's economy, and 3) Its elevator is fixed so all the people can enter the museum safely.

My Grandma Thelma and Grandpa Mose went to the same
 school, right here.
They'd walk up opposite sides of Exodus Drive.
Now, we are beside their house. This is a field where their school
used to be. It's where my ma forgets
she ever harvested squash.

Down Jackson Village Road, up and at the bend
across from the candy lady's blue house, just before that big
 magnolia
is where my Grandma Lizzie and Granddaddy Silas were married.
This iron ochre tub in my parent's front yard is where
my daddy took hogs to slaughter when he was nine.

Less than a mile from here is a creek
where my kin disembark with fish rods,
cold beer, and jokes.
It's where I'll be ashes spread across the Black River.

This is where people put flowers and crosses
for whoever died at the crossroads. They call it respecting the dead.
At the crossroad of Exodus Drive and Jackson Village Road
is where I saw my first live alligator washed up from a hurricane,

playing dead. I watched folks gather
from four directions of the village for food.

Here, still, is 300 acres of white-owned land
where my ancestors were people
called *booming rice industry.*
Yes, Bienvenue means "Welcome" in French.
Yes, this is called Benvenue plantation.
Just down the road is Chicora Wood plantation,
where the first U.S. white woman planter who did not plant
is honored by a plaque and her collections of my ancestors'
   narratives.

It's where my great-great-granddaddy Friday is buried,
and it's where I cannot go without permission.
It's where I went on field trips and screamed
with joy as my soft body flew down acres of wild water
slides over the smoothest grasses I'd ever seen

          where I tried to be a child

spinning around a May pole

          and I let my feet lift off the ground

                    just a bit.

RECORDKEEPER

When I visit cypress-kneed plantations on riverside back roads,
I ask the real Planter Class to tell me their names.
I go, and I tell all my dead to let loose,
to transcend illegible death. I know
I come from the real Planter Class:

this kind more likely to rise up
this kind more likely to take their own life
this kind more likely to take ours

I come from somewhere before writing, before lists.
In South Carolina, lists run long,
and I am from a list of unknowns.

Beneath my feet are children.
Beloved and blooming white clovers,
a rooted song of fungi protecting my every step.

I know I come from the real planters. Real dark. Grave people.
My great-great-granddaddy Friday's cerulean
hands inside dirt life, not beating the Earth
for indigo, cotton, and rice industries.

I drive to Winyah Bay and watch a ship from 1526 roll in with nightingales
painted on its starboard. My great-great-greats are exalted
inside the international paper mill's cloud.
They tell me not to be afraid to go far and find love.
So, I go.

SHIFTING SHAPE

The shade trees are where I find my brother's body
when he's been gone all day long.
We have the same smile.

When we drink Crown Royal,
our uncle's heartbeats
slow down inside of our chest.

We get silly.
Sometimes,
we are outright mean.

I don't know how many of my uncles were found drunk,
frozen to death beneath an oak or cypress,
under branches forgiving as a purple tobacco field.

I went to Paris to learn more about poetry
so I wouldn't kill myself.
I found pine trees, my shadow,
and five pints of beer a night.
Poisonous flowers tending
to all the kin I carry inside of me.

One night I couldn't walk so I called an Uber driver
who called me *Silly American* because the metro he dropped me at
was around the corner. I learned that in France
we were not Black, and I was not his sister.

I couldn't be seen this way.
There were no shade trees to seek.
It was the first time. I was a single
cardinal crossing the Atlantic.
I wanted to die, so I flew.

GRANDDADDY'S TOOLS

I am thirty-three
the first time

I put my hands on a shovel
the first time

I feel my dead
granddaddy alive inside me
I am digging a hole

to put me in with granddaddy's shovel
daddy yells for me to stop
lying in the middle of granddaddy's field

of grasses he says the moisture will make me
sick but my ears have a new fear filter

I am listening to Spirit
I am not dying today.

GRAIN MEMORY

A wishbone branch falls
from my Grandma Thelma's oak
for me.

What do you know about magic? E asks.

E bends e old body down, turns
the wishbone branch into
a cross, places it around my neck.
I am strapped at the Black River's right shoulder,
remembering my Grandpa Mose never wore anything
but church.

My purple head begins to feel
cold as clergy, parched. I ask for water.
E gives me water and rice, says to repeat
after em:
I am fly from nature. Nature fly. I am fly from

nature. Nature

fly. *I am fly from nature.* *Nature*

fly. I am fly

from nature. Nature fly. I am

fly from nature. Nature fly. I am fly from nature. Nature fly.

Ah, I get it! It's an affirmation, I say

and e laughs in windoceansongs.

E whispers, *do not be trapped by language.*

E voice begins to beat my chest
cavity in rhythm, chaff threshed from grain,
separating me from need.

I thought I'd snapped that wishbone branch myself. No.

I am fly from nature. Nature fly.

At dusk,
gleaming marigolds gathered
beneath my feet, singing:

We were stolen shipped across the Atlantic

invasive is a word I heard

stolen thrash thrash thrash and we speak in bloom

PARIS, 2019

I lost control
following cigarette processionals, in and out,
of a freedom-spatting
mausoleum head. I love

James Baldwin.

There are entire worlds
in his words. My heart became
a jade toad, croaking fire. I leapt—
followed e smoke.

AT A 24-HOUR BAR IN NEW ORLEANS AN ANONYMOUS HUMAN TELLS ME E WANTS TO DIE

E hair was stringy and perfect.
E dog's copper coat lit up the dark room.
While reading e friend's poem to me,
e began to cry,
pushing e beer to the side.
I watched air pass
between e teeth and tongue.
E mouth was a living temple.
I didn't know e name.
I thought to myself, *what does it mean to witness?*
To be present?
                An answer fell from the already dying
live oak, sheltering us as our conversation moved
onto the outside patio of lights. I watch trees give life
to dying neighbors without losing their own form.
Another answer falls from the oak's canker sore,
and I listen to the intelligence of trees. Presence.
I told em I wanted to begin gardening,
to watch hard browns, soft greens,
deepen into the earth
like a child's time capsule,
like how strange it was to have met while alive
in a famed city of bones.

WA E GO OVA DAT BIG OL WATA FA?

—Grandma Thelma

I wanted to find James Baldwin's signature
and touch it while standing in the city
where e body walked. I began searching
for the Abbey Bookstore in Paris.

When I finally found the place,
I found my Grandpa Mose's daddy, Papa,
shimmering in chartreuse,
suspended mid-air and surrounded by books.

E was reading
Césaire, Fanon, and Ida B. Wells while sipping
a bit of my Grandma Thelma's
muscadine wine dug up from the dirt.

I'd only seen Papa in photographs. His smile
was so familiar, I almost didn't see
the red, white, and blue flags, hanging
above the bookstore entryway:
French, American, and Canadian.

I did see the colors blurring
before my eyes, my breath frigid
and picking up pace in my chest. My eyes searching
for the big battle X that will not die.

I forgot I was in Paris
until Papa began to sing, wide and deep
as the Atlantic, *Go down, Moses, way down…*

Papa, I walked with my shadow
along the Seine River and e didn't speak my name.
I walked with my shadow along the Black River, turns out
e always knew my name.

When I got back, my ma handed me a book called,
Ebony Effects: 150 Unknown Facts about Blacks in Georgetown, S.C.,
and e couldn't wait to show me your smiling face,
and I touched it with my fingers.

HOME BODY

My bones
are not just my own.

I feed them honey, oranges,
copper, and crystals. I clear my soul.

My skeletal holds a mouthful of mundane
magic. I come from everywhere. My words go
everywhere. The wind always brings me back my first face.

A red serpent circles my feet,
forming itself into infinity. There, another bloody October moon.
I am watching

pine trees pick up their roots
and walk.

PINE TREE

I was sitting inside my 2006 Saturn Vue
in my parent's garage, and you calmed me.

You are the same tree
that knew me, then. Myself.

I was a bleeding child inside. My purple
ideas were smashed silent by Grandpa Mose's fists.
Now, you are bruised and missing pieces of yourself.
Somehow you are still standing outside, rooted.

Alive. I know I need to see you this way,
to see myself more clearly.

You are your own behind my granddaddy Silas's
fading red fence, needling the sky's breath. Medicine,

you are woodworking. With all my reverence I praise
your knotted parts. I ask
permission to cut

your needles, to boil them.
I ask you to bless my new home.

MEMORIES OF EMOTIONAL LABOR

While taking the recycling bin out
to the front yard,
I can hear my ma's voice, clear
as a pileated woodpecker,
knocking the catalpa.
Today, I need you to—
Listen to my feelings
Tell me you love me
Lie next to me while I watch this movie
Do the laundry
I'm nine years old,
and I don't want
to do the laundry.

When the recycling bin empties,
I bring it back inside.
I walk past the dishes
in my sink,

and I hear my daddy call
from 20 years ago.
I respond and e says
nothing,

which means
I'm supposed to go
and see what e needs.
Today, I need you to—

Tell your mama I love em
Stop crying all the time
Write something to your ma in this card for me
Take up all the weeds in the front bed

I'm 14 years old,
and I don't care
about the weeds in the flower bed.

I'm 34 years old
and I'm watching *Ghostwriter*
for research. One of my favorite TV shows
I didn't remember from childhood.

Fuck the dishes, I say to no one,
as I place my phone on Do Not Disturb.

My dog has things e needs me to do,
but it won't disrupt my blooming.

THE MADNESS THAT UNCHAINS ITSELF

in the dark is the largest lighthouse in South Carolina
built by enslaved people with names
called by others madness
old-world hands tightening around my throat
I climbed a mountain of not's for years
wet my mouth on lonely stone
I jumped into a dead waterfall
where a river stopped and stood
still to greet my face
we made love in that dark
space between a dream and an idea

madness is the punch I knew
the kiss I thought I needed

my own water wetting my private parts
dried in someone else's sun
I swallowed bloody moons to remember home
whole worlds to forget my own
I felt dumb when I didn't know
everything you did
though I knew more than most around me
by the age of 12 I couldn't
throw over a table if I wanted to
even if it was blasphemy
we were talking about

madness has its own medicine
its own trails to follow and know

I'm going into all my shadows
here's all I thought I couldn't hold
what I've become for now, knowing
I'll dive again
be made new

IF YOU REALLY REAL, YOU'D JUMP OFF THIS BRIDGE WITH US, FOR US

I am carrying faith in a bronze bucket   down every road

in my right hand faith sloshes   as I step forward

step backward or to the side   a misstep

I am carrying faith as far as I can   take it to feed dream vines

to wake ruptured hearts   I carry faith

like it's oxygen   like I must make it to wherever I am going

wherever I am going   I am carrying faith

in my gut is a field   down a white rocky road a yellow sun

haloing my head   in my throat

growing louder and louder in my head something said,

you come from the stick you hold

I am carrying faith up mountains across valleys of bones and cries

no pulpit   I am carrying faith in a bronze bucket

carrying water   weighted air

NOTES & RESEARCH

- "Look out for me I'm a-coming, too" and "Glory into my soul" are lines borrowed from the song, "I Am Bound for De Kingdom," composed by Florence Price & sung by Marian Anderson
- "If Anybody Asks You What's the Matter with Me" is a line borrowed from the gospel song, "Running for My Life"
- "A Rose" remixes lines borrowed from the gospel song, "He Rose from the Dead", especially a particular rendition included on the album, *John's Island, South Carolina: Its People & Songs*
- "Negro Friend" borrows from *My Negro Friends* by Genevieve Chandler in Plantersville, South Carolina (https://www.loc.gov/resource/wpalh3.30050407/) from the *U.S. Work Projects Administration, Federal Writers' Project: Folklore Project, Life Histories, 1936-39*
- "~~Pre~~face" borrows from *A Goodly Heritage*, a pamphlet produced by The Rice Museum (Georgetown, SC) in 1972
- In Gullah-Geechee culture, "e/em" are gender-neutral pronouns.
- *The Heart Sutra*, as recited in the Triratna Buddhist Community
- *The Holy Bible*, The Books of Ecclesiastes, Ephesians, and Psalms
- *Dear Universe* by Yolo Akili
- *The Black Interior* by Elizabeth Alexander
- *Bless Me, Ultima* by Rudolfo Anaya
- *A Map to the Door of No Return: Notes to Belonging* by Dionne Brand
- Kamau Brathwaite's Bibliography (https://www.zotero.org groups/304824/kamau_brathwaite_bibliography)
- *Return to My Native Land* by Aimé Césaire
- CA Conrad's Bibliography
- *A Far Cry from Plymouth Rock* by Kwame Dawes
- *Gullah Branches: West African Roots* by Ronald Daise
- *Acupressure for Emotional Healing* by Michael Reed Gach & Beth Ann Henning

- *Pluto: The Evolutionary Journey of the Soul* by Jeff Green
- *Gullah Images: The Art of Jonathan Green* by Jonathan Green
- Nikky Finney's Bibliography
- *The Power of the Porch: The Storyteller's Craft in Zora Neale Hurston, Gloria Naylor, and Randall Kenan* by Trudier Harris
- *Siddhartha* by Herman Hesse
- Hopsewee Plantation, Gullah or Black-led tour
- "Poetics" from *Keywords in African American Studies* by Meta DuEwa Jones
- *Down by the Riverside: A South Carolina Slave Community* by Charles Joyner
- *The Hoodoo Tarot: 78-Card Deck and Book for Rootworkers* by Tayannah Lee McQuillar
- *Woman, Native, Other* by Trinh T. Minh-ha
- *The Wounded Healer* by Henri J. M. Nouwen
- *A Glossary of Haunting* by Eve Tuck and C. Ree
- The Rice Museum, Gullah or Black-led tour
- *Root Magic* by Eden Royce
- Sandy Island, The Joyner Institute for Gullah & African Diaspora Studies
- *The Healing Wisdom of Africa* by Malidoma Patrice Somé
- *Tao Te Ching* by Lao Tzu
- *Ebony Effects: 150 Unknown Facts about Blacks in Georgetown, S.C.* by Steve Williams

ACKNOWLEDGMENTS

I express immense gratitude to the following people and community arts organizations—

to the literary journals and magazines where some of these poems first appeared in their original versions:

"The Shade Tree" and "Pine Tree" were first published by *Annulet: A Journal of Poetics*, 2022

"I Am Bound for De Kingdom" was first published by the *Oxford American*, 2021

"Hurricane Family" was first published by *Moist Poetry Journal*, 2021

"Plantersville, South Carolina" was first published by the *Southern Humanities Review*, 2021

"If Anybody Asks You What's the Matter with Me" and "A Rose" were first published by *OROBORO*, 2021

"Grain Memory," "Perhaps I Am A Fugitive of Empathy," and "My Grandma Told Stories or Cautionary Tales" were first published by *POETRY*, 2021

"Recordkeeper" was first published in *Emergence Magazine*, 2021

"Granddaddy's Tools" was first published in *Root Work Journal*, 2020

for their support while I was conducting research for this manuscript and building the workshop(s) that accompany the complete work:

God, Spirit, my respected ancestors, Vernetta Dekine, Tom Dekine, Tamara Tucker, Tomeika Dekine, Trevor Dekine, Joseph Dekine, Linda and Henry Smith, Kennedy Funny,

Jazmin Black Grollemund, Ellen Clement, Max Lit, Krista E. Hughes, Cassandra Byrd, Jason Spencer, Davelyn Hill, Queen and Ray Funnye, Dominique Vedrine, Ian Morris, Charmell Davis, Lauren Quevedo, Susan Prestipino, Shemuel Namaste, Crystal Irby, Susan Ledford Lea, Courtney Leak, Markiesha Nesbitt, Michelle, Natalie and Sara Daise, Scott Neely, Norman Williamson, Marquita Littleton, Cedric Umoja, Eric Kocher, Cody Owens, Celestial Poet, Ann Jones, Zenobia Harper, Virginia Flanagan, Carmelita Byrd, Khrystie Stefin, Veronica Skinner, Lesley Quast, Weston Milliken, Shay Black, Nicole Hazard, Lydia Clarridge, Fire, Hilary Keane, Calvin Byrd, Glenis Redmond, Kimbi the Goddess, Lynn Casteel Harper, Ryan Harper, Caroline Caldwell, Traci Barr, Erin Hahn, Antoinette Palmer, Anna Abhau Elliot, Maria Swearingen, Sheree Angela Matthews, Gender Benders, the South Carolina Arts Commission, Speaking Down Barriers, Alternate Roots, and many others since 1986.

for reading and listening to my work with careful consideration and insight:

Tyree Daye, Gabrielle Calvocoressi, Denise Duhamel, Suzanne Cleary, and the Low-Residency MFA Cohort at Converse University, Nick Laird, Ishion Hutchinson, and the Low-Residency MFA Cohort at New York University in Paris, noor ibn najam, Shakeema Smalls, Destiny Hemphill, Eden Royce, Kwame Dawes, Ron Daise, Cameron Awkward Rich, and the 2021 Tin House Winter Workshop, Terrance Hayes, Danez Smith, Delana Dameron and the 2017 Cohort at The Watering

Hole, Andrew Simonet, Ce Scott-Fitz, Michaela Pilar-Brown, and the ArtistsU Big Projects Club.

for publishing this manuscript with care and ingenuity:
Meg Reid, Kate McMullen, and the Hub City Press team.

MARLANDA DEKINE (they/she) is a poet and author obsessed with ancestry, memory, and the process of staying within one's own body. Their work leaves spells and incantations for others to follow for themselves. Dekine is the author of the self-published collection and mixtape, *i am from a punch & a kiss*. Their poems have been published or are forthcoming in the *Poetry Out Loud Anthology, POETRY Magazine, Emergence Magazine, Southern Humanities Review, Oxford American*, and elsewhere. Dekine is a Tin House Own Path Scholar. They live in South Carolina with their wise dog, Malachi.

HUB CITY PRESS is a non-profit independent press in Spartanburg, SC that publishes well-crafted, high-quality works by new and established authors, with an emphasis on the Southern experience. We are committed to high-caliber novels, short stories, poetry, plays, memoir, and works emphasizing regional culture and history. We are particularly interested in books with a strong sense of place.

Hub City Press is an imprint of the non-profit Hub City Writers Project, founded in 1995 to foster a sense of community through the literary arts. Our metaphor of organization purposely looks backward to the nineteenth century when Spartanburg was known as the "hub city," a place where railroads converged and departed.

The New Southern Voices Book Prize was established in 2013 and is a biennial prize awarded to an emerging Southern poet who has published at most one previous collection of poetry. It is awarded for a book-length collection of poems written originally in English.

PREVIOUS WINNERS

2019: Megan Denton Ray *Mustard, Milk, and Gin*

2017: Lindsey Alexander *Rodeo in Reverse*

2015: J.K. Daniels *Wedding Pulls*

2013: Lilah Hegnauer *Pantry*

CPSIA information can be obtained
at www.ICGtesting.com
Printed in the USA
JSHW020309280222
23420JS00005B/5

9 781938 235948